MOONSTONE ·○· JET ·○· EMERALD ·○· AMETHYST ·○· CORAL ·○· PEARL ·○· TOURMALINE ·○· PERIDOT ·○·

And deep-brained sonnets, that did amplify
Each stone's dear nature, worth, and quality.

from A Lover's Complaint
William Shakespeare

...and jewels five-words long
That on the stretched forefinger of All Time
Sparkle for ever.

from The Princess, part II, l 355
Alfred Lord Tennyson

Strings of Pearls

A collection of poems

LAUTUS PRESS

Also published by Lautus Press:

Washing Lines: A collection of poems
selected by Janie Hextall and Barbara McNaught

This collection was first published in 2013 by Lautus Press
Ryton House, Lechlade, GL7 3AR

ISBN: 978-0-9568265-1-0

© Janie Hextall and Barbara McNaught 2013

Designed and typeset in Minion Pro by Touchmedia, Cheltenham
Printed by Berforts Information Press, Eynsham

A CIP catalogue record for this book is available from the British Library

Contents

Robert Graves *The Necklace*	8
Helen Dunmore *Greek Beads*	9
Kathleen Jamie *The Brooch*	10
Menna Elfyn *Brooch*	11
Robert Herrick *A Ring Presented to Julia*	12
George Crabbe *A Marriage Ring*	12
Inscription inside a watch	13
Eithne Cavanagh *The Necklace*	14
Gillian Clarke *Amber*	15
Colette Bryce *The Wearer*	16
Julie O'Callaghan *Opals*	18
Alicia Stubbersfield *Jane's Pearls*	19
Moniza Alvi *Presents from my Aunts in Pakistan*	20
Simon Armitage *from The Book of Matches*	22
Victoria Redel *Bedecked*	23
Ted Hughes *The Locket*	24
Edna St Vincent Millay *The Courage That My Mother Had*	26
Grevel Lindop *My Grandmother's Opal*	27
William Strode *A Necklace*	28
Carol Ann Duffy *Warming her Pearls*	29
Emily Dickinson *I held a jewel*	30
Chang Chi *The Chaste Wife's Reply*	31
H D *The Flowering of the Rod*	32
Robert Louis Stevenson *I Will Make You Brooches*	34
Arthur Weir *A Mother's Jewels*	35
T S Eliot *A Game of Chess*	36
William Shakespeare *from A Lover's Complaint*	37
Jane Draycott *Pearl*	38
Eithne Cavanagh *A Beading of Words*	41

Traditional *Nursery Rhymes*	42
Louisa May Alcott *Here is the Bracelet*	43
Christina Rossetti *Precious Stones*	44
Dorothy Parker *The Choice*	45
Traditional *Birthstones*	46
C P Cavafy *For the Shop*	48
James Fenton *Nothing*	49
Sally Evans *Whitby Jet*	50
Gillian Clarke *Welsh Gold*	51
Fleur Adcock *Blue Glass*	52
Robert Graves *The Uncut Diamond*	54
Elizabeth Jennings *The Diamond Cutter*	55
Alfred Teynnyson *from Morte d'Arthur*	56
Geoffrey Chaucer *from Romaunt of the Rose*	57
Carol Ann Duffy *Rings*	58
Robert Graves *A Lost Jewel*	60
Sally Evans *Brooch Found at Redcar*	61
John Keats *from The Eve of St Agnes*	62
Thomas Moore *Rich and Rare Were the Gems She Wore*	63
Ruth Fainlight *Nacre*	64
Kit Wright *In Memory of a Beautiful Jeweller*	66
Leysa Lowery *String of Pearls*	67
Robert Graves *A Bracelet*	68
Sarah Maguire *The Invisible Mender (My First Mother)*	69
Alice Walker *We Alone*	70
Harold Monro *Overheard on a Saltmarsh*	71
Tess Gallagher *from Two Bracelets*	72
Matthew Francis *Of Diamonds*	73
Robert Herrick *The Bracelet: To Julia*	74

Homer *from The Odyssey* (trans by Robert Fagles)   75
Robert Melliard *Jewellery*   76
Sasha Moorsom *Jewels in my hand*   77

Illustrations

Harry Brockway *The Pearl Necklace*   8
C R Ashbee *Chain necklace with peacock pendant*   17
A New Guinea Dandy, wood engraving, 1895   22
Baroness Burdett-Coutts, wood engraving, c 1900   26
Philip Gregory Needell *Woman at Kitchen Table*   34
Josie Brown *Necklace of Jewels*   40
Daisy Chain   43
Lucien Métivet *Les Bijoux*   44
Jean de Mandeville *Jeweller's Shop* from Le Lapidaire   48
Anita Klein *Angel with Black Necklace*   53
Dante Gabriel Rossetti *King Arthur and the Weeping Queens*   56
Alice Patullo *Pearly King and Queen*   68
Atelier Trias *Art Deco Lady*   72
Muhammad Abed *Portrait of Shah Jahan holding a jewel*   79

Small jewel illustrations

From Victorian Jewellery, Studio Editions 1991:
page 13 Fine Diamond Double Heart and Knot No 21,463 (Goldsmiths & Silversmiths Co Ltd 1901)
page 25 Solid Gold Side Locket, Satin, No 1008 (S F Myers & Co 1894)
page 37 Gold bracelet No 987 (Saunders & Shepherd Ltd 1903-4)
page 54 Fine Diamond Maltese Cross Pendant No 21,546 (Goldsmiths & Silversmiths Co Ltd 1901)
page 59 Ladies' Guard Ring 2606 (Mappin & Webb Ltd 1900)
page 74 Necklet No 2348 (Saunders & Shepherd Ltd 1903-4)

From Antique "Schmucksachen", Ancient Jewellery, German Lithograph (Book 14 of the 4th edition of Meyers Konversationslexikon 1885–90 Bibliographisches Institut in Leipzig):
page 30 Anhänger (*pendant*), von H. Holbein d. jüng. entworfen (27)
page 61 Fibula (*brooch/cloak pin*) von Tuttlingen (19)
page 66 Indischer Halsschmuck (*necklace*) (23)

The Necklace
Robert Graves (1895-1985)

Variegated flowers, nuts, cockle-shells
And pebbles, chosen lovingly and strung
On golden spider-webs with a gold clasp
For your neck, naturally: and each bead touched

By a child's lips as he stoops over them:
Wear these for the new miracle they announce –
All four cross-quarter-days beseech you –
Your safe return from shipwreck, drought and war,
Beautiful as before, to what you are.

Greek Beads

Helen Dunmore

Small, silvery, slipping
from finger to finger,
beads for street corners,

beads for white noon
when shadows curl by the walls
and the dog in the square lolls
with his tongue unfurled,

beads for navy-blue evenings
when the smell of oranges
drifts to the fountain,

beads for waiting on the landing-stage,
for the heat that shimmers
from village to village,

for the boy guarding the goats
and the old woman hoeing in black,
beads for leaving to find work
and for the dream of coming back,

beads for remembering
and for forgetting,
wrapped round the wrists of babies
and the dying,

beads for the life we live in,
small, silvery, slipping
from finger to finger.

The Brooch
Kathleen Jamie

All I have is small enough
to be held in one hand –
an agate brooch. It's pierced

like an implement or tool,
perhaps a loom weight.
The agates are brindled,

grey, like carded wool,
or the rings inside a cup, drained,
set to be washed on a table.

Of the woman who pinned it
to her plain coat, only this remains:
her gift, my heirloom, stones.

Brooch

Menna Elfyn
translated from the Welsh by Elin ap Hywel
in memory of Stephanie Macleod

They have their place, accessories:
earrings, the odd necklace,
gemstone bracelets...
and yet, it's from the soft inner depth
we work the brooch of our lives,
that jewelled keepsake set to outlast us.
Yours, it was a brooch ablaze –
the passion-crafted clasp,
the light chain to keep it safe;
others, now, will wear your brooch –
this jewel fashioned from a golden heart.
It will catch the sun. It will dazzle us.

A Ring Presented to Julia
Robert Herrick (1591-1674)

Julia, I bring
To thee this ring,
Made for thy finger fit;
To show by this
That our love is
(Or should be) like to it.
...
And as this round
Is nowhere found
To flaw, or else to sever;
So let our love
As endless prove,
And pure as gold for ever.

A Marriage Ring
George Crabbe (1754-1832)

The ring, so worn as you behold,
So thin, so pale, is yet of gold:
The passion such it was to prove–
Worn with life's care, love yet was love.

This inscription from inside a watch of 1630 was engraved as a lover's knot inside the lid of the watch case

This is love and worth commending
Still beginning - never ending;
Like a withy nett insnaring
In a round shuts up all squaring
In and out, whose every angle
More and more doth still entangle
Keeps a measure still in moving
And is never light but loving
Twining arms exchanging kisses
Each partaking others blisses
Laughing, weeping still together
Bliss in one is mirth in either
Never breaking ever bending
This is love and worth commending.

The Necklace
Eithne Cavanagh

Each bead holds a tiny galaxy,
bubbles trapped forever
in hard clean roundness.

I still have the necklace
that you bought for me in Florence.
Its coppery orbs evoke the glass
my father candle-smoked
preparing for an eclipse.

I love the imperfection of the beads
and hold one high against the sun.
A shimmer frills the edge,
creates a dazzling halo.

The metal links still hold.
The clasp remains as strong
as on that languid night
you placed the beads around my neck,
a time of hope and tears.

Today my eyes need no shade.
Feelings fall like molten stars
and settle - a clear glazed sheet
with you in perfect focus.

Amber
Gillian Clarke

Coveted week after week on the market stall,
coiled, nonchalant, arrayed under the lid
of locked glass, they grew familiar.
She'd finger them, slip them over her head,
try them for size, spoilt for choice –
red-amber, yellow, cut Russian ruby,
or those sad rosaries, widow's beads of Whitby jet.
In each bead surfaced the cloudy face of a woman.

Warmed by the sunlight on dressing tables,
or against a woman's skin, then laid safe
in a drawer each night between the silk leaves
of her underwear. Never cold, as if
each bead were an unquenchable flame
that burned a million years like a sanctuary lamp
beneath the ice, each drip of sticky gold
hardening to honeyed stone.

As if nothing that has ever contained heat
can be cold again, mirrors never empty
and our rooms, furniture, hoarded amulets,
could reassemble themselves into a life
and still pass hand to hand from underneath
the permafrost, ice woman to living daughter.

The Wearer
Colette Bryce

Here is my necklace, blister
pearls, a single garnet
for the eye, diamond sparks,
but where am I?

This loop contained a laugh,
a pulse, a throat
that arched perhaps
in love, perhaps
disdain, that warmed
this chain and knew
itself as beautiful.

Whoosh ... life! A peacock tail
can stop a clock, can shock
a room to silence.
Oh I played that game,
observed the trembling
hands of men pause
above my breasts. Exquisite,
they would murmur then.

Feast your eyes, look
for me. You'll find
my books, my silverware,
my gowns, the flute
that held my wine, the fork
that carried food
to my full lips.
The set, the props, and this,

this ... my vanity, that loved
the gaze that looked
at me, that bloomed
like any peacock tail
at the soft words
of a lover, who whispered
that my teeth were pearls,
my ear a shell, mother-
of-pearl, that sapphires
were my eyes

but where am I?

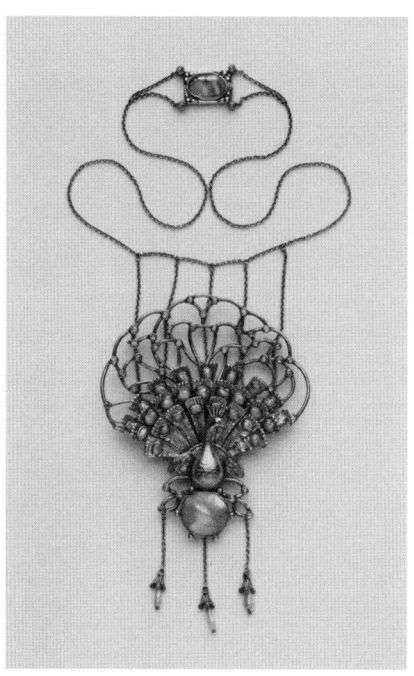

Colette's poem was inspired by a peacock-shaped necklace designed in 1901 by Charles Robert Ashbee (1863–1942), one of the earliest Arts and Crafts jewellery designers. Ashbee believed that the value of jewellery lay in its design, not in the monetary value of the materials used. Although this peacock jewel is one of his more sumptuous creations, it would have been modest in price compared with the heavy, diamond-set jewellery of other designers of the period.

Opals
Julie O'Callaghan

Lying on my stomach,
silk pillows underneath me,
I trace the outline
of each plum blossom
on my sleeve
and try to hide my face
from the other ladies
with the screen of my hair.
They are discussing the Prince,
gossiping about which royal robe
suits him best.
I have traced the flower six times now,
hoping they won't ask me my opinion
or notice the handful of opal teardrops
decorating my sleeve.

Jane's Pearls
Alicia Stubbersfield

Rochester called her all day
like you would a dog or cat,
up and down corridors, behind
curtains and in the orchard
where only the owls answered.

The second night he put candles in
her room, opened wardrobes, drawers,
found nothing he'd given to her gone.
He picked up a narrow, suede box,
flicked its little gold catch.

Pearls curled round themselves,
a slight bloom like an apricot.
Each bead different from the next,
each pearl a supplication in his hands,
a rosary he could tell to bring her back.

It fitted round his neck,
hidden under his cravat.
The diamond clasp fixed.
Pearls cool against his sallow skin,
the touch of fingertips at his throat.

Presents from my Aunts in Pakistan
Moniza Alvi

They sent me a salwar kameez
             peacock-blue,
                          and another
          glistening like an orange split open,
embossed slippers, gold and black
                points curling.
         Candy-striped glass bangles
                       snapped, drew blood.
         Like at school, fashions changed
                in Pakistan –
the salwar bottoms were broad and stiff,
                then narrow.
My aunts chose an apple-green sari,
       silver-bordered
                  for my teens.

I tried each satin-silken top –
         was alien in the sitting room.
I could never be as lovely
                as those clothes
       I longed
for denim and corduroy.
         My costume clung to me
                and I was aflame,
I couldn't rise up out of its fire,
       half-English,
                unlike Aunt Jamila.

I wanted my parents' camel-skin lamp –
         switching it on in my bedroom,
to consider the cruelty
             and the transformation
from camel to shade,
       marvel at the colours
                like stained glass.

My mother cherished her jewellery –
    Indian gold, dangling, filigree.
          But it was stolen from our car.
The presents were radiant in my wardrobe.
    My aunts requested cardigans
        from Marks and Spencers.
My salwar kameez
    didn't impress the schoolfriend
who sat on my bed, asked to see
    my weekend clothes.
But often I admired the mirror-work,
    tried to glimpse myself
        in the miniature
glass circles, recall the story
    how the three of us
        sailed to England.
Prickly heat had me screaming on the way.
    I ended up in a cot
in my English grandmother's dining room,
    found myself alone,
        playing with a tin boat.

I pictured my birthplace
    from fifties' photographs.
        When I was older
there was a conflict, a fractured land
    throbbing through newsprint.
Sometimes I saw Lahore –
        my aunts in shaded rooms,
screened from male visitors,
    sorting presents,
        wrapping them in tissue.

Or there were beggars, sweeper-girls
    and I was there –
        of no fixed nationality,
staring through fretwork
        at the Shalimar gardens.

from **The Book of Matches**
Simon Armitage

*

My father thought it bloody queer,
the day I rolled home with a ring of silver in my ear
half hidden by a mop of hair. "You've lost your head.
If that's how easily you're led
you should've had it through your nose instead."

And even then I hadn't had the nerve to numb
the lobe with ice, then drive a needle through the skin,
then wear a safety-pin. It took a jeweller's gun
to pierce the flesh, and then a friend
to thread the sleeper in, and where it slept
the hole became a sore, became a wound, and wept.

At twenty-nine, it comes as no surprise to hear
my own voice breaking like a tear, released like water,
cried from way back in the spiral of the ear. *If I were you,
I'd take it out and leave it out next year.*

A NEW GUINEA DANDY

Bedecked

Victoria Redel

Tell me it's wrong the scarlet nails my son sports or the toy store rings
        he clusters four jewels to each finger.

He's bedecked. I see the other mothers looking at the star choker,
        the rhinestone strand he fastens over a sock.
Sometimes I help him find sparkle clip-ons when he says sticker
        earrings look too fake.
Tell me I should teach him it's wrong to love the glitter that a boy's
        only a boy who'd love a truck with a remote that revs,
battery slamming into corners or Hot Wheels loop-de-looping off
        tracks into the tub.

Then tell me it's fine—really—maybe even a good thing—a boy who's
        got some girl to him,
and I'm right for the days he wears a pink shirt on the seesaw in
        the park.

Tell me what you need to tell me but keep far away from my son
        who still loves a beautiful thing not for what it means—
this way or that—but for the way facets set off prisms and prisms spin
        up everywhere
and from his own jewelled body he's cast rainbows—made every
        shining true colour.

Now try to tell me—man or woman—your heart was ever once
        that brave.

The Locket
Ted Hughes (1930-1998)

Sleeping and waking in the Song of Songs
You were half blissful. But on occasion
Casually as a yawn, you'd open
Your death and contemplate it.

Your death
Was so utterly within your power
It was as if you had trapped it. Maybe by somehow
Giving it some part of you, for its food.

Now it was your curio pet,
Your familiar. But who else would have nursed it
In a locket between her breasts?

Smiling, you'd hold it up.
You'd swing it on its chain, to tease life.
It lent you uncanny power. A secret, blueish,
Demonic flash
When you smiled and gently bit the locket.

I have read how a fiery cross
Can grow and brighten in the dreams of a spinster.
But a crooked key turned in your locket.
It had sealed your door in Berlin
With the brand of the burnt. You knew exactly
How your death looked. It was a long-cold oven
Locked with a swastika.

The locket kept splitting open.
I would close it. You would smile.
It's lips kept coming apart – just a slit.
The clasp seemed to be faulty.
Who could have guessed what it was trying to say?
Your beauty, a folktale wager,
Was a quarter century posthumous.

While I juggled our futures, it kept up its whisper
To my deafened ear: *fait accompli.*

The Courage That My Mother Had

Edna St. Vincent Millay (1892-1950)

The courage that my mother had
Went with her, and is with her still:
Rock from New England quarried;
Now granite in a granite hill.

The golden brooch my mother wore
She left behind for me to wear;
I have no thing I treasure more:
Yet, it is something I could spare.

Oh, if instead she'd left to me

The thing she took into the grave!—
That courage like a rock, which she
Has no more need of, and I have.

My Grandmother's Opal
Grevel Lindop

Nowadays I can find no picture of her.
I lost the only photograph I had
moving house; nothing else came to me,
so all I keep now is this opulent bead,

milky violet, craggy sugar-white
and crumpled goldleaf fused into the one
hurtfully alluring crystal depth
of opal, her favourite stone,

which like a scrying-globe entraps the eye;
though I should need more than a jeweller's glass
to see what figures might flaw the blue mist
or walk unscathed out of that golden furnace,

distant and enigmatic, bright and small
as now my memories of her: some stories
and nonsense-rhymes she riddled me out of her childhood
odd scents she used, her sharp, affectionate gaze,

skirts I buried my face in, and the love
which like an animal I could discern,
inhabit like warmth but never comprehend
or, so young I was, return.

So here it is, my grandmother's opal,
centrepiece of a necklace broken and strewn
who now knows where? And of no use to me,
too large for a ring, too splendid to cut down,

message I can't read, riches not mine
to spend or give, unexplained trust I hold.
I keep it: but where shall I set it, this one spark
saved from the fiery heart of a lost world?

A Necklace
William Strode (1598-1645)

These veines are nature's nett,
These cords by art are sett.

If love himselfe flye here,
Love is intangled here.

Loe! on my neck this twist I bind,
For to hang him that steales my mynde:
Unless hee hang alive in chaynes
I hang and dye in lingring paynes.

Theis threads enjoy a double grace,
Both by the gemme and by the place.

Warming Her Pearls

Carol Ann Duffy
for Judith Radstone

Next to my own skin, her pearls. My mistress
bids me wear them, warm them, until evening
when I'll brush her hair. At six, I place them
round her cool, white throat. All day I think of her,

resting in the Yellow Room, contemplating silk
or taffeta, which gown tonight? She fans herself
whilst I work willingly, my slow heat entering
each pearl. Slack on my neck, her rope.

She's beautiful. I dream about her
in my attic bed; picture her dancing
with tall men, puzzled by my faint, persistent scent
beneath her French perfume, her milky stones.
I dust her shoulders with a rabbit's foot,
watch the soft blush seep through her skin
like an indolent sigh. In her looking-glass
my red lips part as though I want to speak.

Full moon. Her carriage brings her home. I see
her every movement in my head ... Undressing,
taking off her jewels, her slim hand reaching
for the case, slipping naked into bed, the way

she always does ... And I lie here awake,
knowing the pearls are cooling even now
in the room where my mistress sleeps. All night
I feel their absence and I burn.

I held a jewel

Emily Dickinson (1830-1886)

I held a jewel in my fingers
And went to sleep
The day was warm, and winds were prosy
I said, "Twill keep"

I woke - and chide my honest fingers,
The Gem was gone
And now, an Amethyst remembrance
Is all I own

The Chaste Wife's Reply

Chang Chi (Tang Dynasty)
Translated by Herbert A Giles (1845-1935)

Knowing, fair Sir, my matrimonial thrall,
Two pearls thou sentest me, costly withal.
And I, seeing that love thy heart possessed,
I wrapped them coldly in my silken vest.

For mine is a household of high degree,
My husband captain in the King's army;
And me with wit like thine should say,
The troth of wives is forever and aye.

With thy two pearls, I send thee back two tears:
Tears - that we did not meet in earlier years.

The Flowering of the Rod (28)
from **Trilogy**
H.D. (1886-1961)

and Kaspar saw as in a mirror,
another head uncovered and two crowned,

one with a plain circlet, one with a circlet of gems
which even he could not name;

and Kaspar, master of caravans,
had known splendours such as few have known,

and seen jewels cut and un-cut that altered
like water at sun-rise and sun-set,

and blood-stones and sapphires;
we need no detailed statement of Kaspar's specific knowledge

nor inventory of his own possessions,
all we need to know is that Kaspar

knew more about precious stones than any other,
more even than Balthazar;

but his heart was filled with more exalted ecstasy
than any valuer over a new tint of rose or smoke grey

in an Indian opal or pearl; this was Kaspar
who saw as in a mirror,

one head uncrowned and then one with a plain head-band
and then one with a circlet of gems of an inimitable colour;

they were blue yet verging on purple,
yet very blue; if asked to describe them,

you would say they were blue stones
of a curious square cut and set so that the light

broke as if from within; the reflecting inner facets
seemed to cast incalculable angles of light,

this blue shot with violet;
how convey what he felt?

he saw as in a mirror, clearly, O very clearly,
a circlet of square-cut stones on the head of a lady,

and what he saw made his heart so glad
that it was as if he suffered,

his heart laboured so
with his ecstasy.

I Will Make You Brooches

Robert Louis Stevenson (1850-1894)

I will make you brooches and toys for your delight
Of bird-song at morning and star-shine at night.
I will make a palace fit for you and me,
Of green days in forests and blue days at sea.

I will make my kitchen, and you shall keep your room,
Where white flows the river and bright blows the broom,
And you shall wash your linen and keep your body white
In rainfall at morning and dewfall at night.

And this shall be for music when no one else is near,
The fine song for singing, the rare song to hear!
That only I remember, that only you admire,
Of the broad road that stretches and the roadside fire.

A Mother's Jewels

Arthur Weir (1864-1902)

The daughter of a hundred earls,
No jewels has with mine to mate,
Though she may wear in flawless pearls
The ransom of a mighty state.

Hers glitter for the world to see,
But chill the breast where they recline:
My jewels warmly compass me,
And all their brilliancy is mine.

My diamonds are my baby's eyes,
His lips, sole rubies that I crave:
They came to me from Paradise,
And not through labors of the slave.

My darling's arms my necklace make,
'Tis Love that links his feeble hands,
And Death, alone, that chain can break,
And rob me of those priceless bands.

II A Game of Chess
from **The Waste Land**
T S Eliot (1888-1965)

The Chair she sat in, like a burnished throne,
Glowed on the marble, where the glass
Held up by standards wrought with fruited vines
From which a golden Cupidon peeped out
(Another hid his eyes behind his wing)
Doubled the flames of sevenbranched candelabra
Reflecting light upon the table as
The glitter of her jewels rose to meet it,
From satin cases poured in rich profusion.
In vials of ivory and coloured glass
Unstoppered, lurked her strange synthetic perfumes,
Unguent, powdered, or liquid—troubled, confused
And drowned the sense in odours; stirred by the air
That freshened from the window, these ascended
In fattening the prolonged candle-flames,
Flung their smoke into the laquearia,
Stirring the pattern on the coffered ceiling.
Huge sea-wood fed with copper
Burned green and orange, framed by the coloured stone,
In which sad light a carvèd dolphin swam.

from **A Lover's Complaint**
William Shakespeare (1564-1616)

And lo! behold these talents of their hair,
with twisted metal amorously impleached,
I have received from many a several fair,
Their kind acceptance weepingly beseeched,
With the annexions of fair gems enriched,
And deep-brained sonnets, that did amplify
Each stone's dear nature, worth, and quality.

The diamond; why, 'twas beautiful and hard,
Whereto his invised properties did tend;
The deep-green emerald, in whose fresh regard
Weak sights their sickly radiance do amend;
The heaven-hued sapphire and the opal blend
With objects manifold: each several stone,
With wit well blazoned, smiled, or made some moan.

Pearl (IV)

A medieval elegy translated by Jane Draycott

Then fiercer than longing came the fear.
I didn't stir or dare to call
to her: wide-eyed and silent as a hawk
in a great hall I waited there.
I knew that what I saw was spirit
and I feared for what might follow –
that within my sight she'd disappear
before I could come close to her.
So smooth, so small, so delicate,
this graceful innocent girl now rose
before me in her royal robes,
a precious creature set with pearls.

Then like a vision granted, showered
in pearls fit for a princess or a queen
this child as fresh as a lily-flower
stepped down toward the stream.
The fine white linen she wore seemed woven
with light, its side-panels loose and flowing
and laced with borders of seed pearls lovelier
than any I'd ever seen before.
The sleeves of her robe fell long and low,
stitched in with double rows of pearls.
Her skirts of the same fine linen were trimmed
and seeded all over with precious gems.

The girl wore one thing more: a crown
composed entirely of ice-bright pearls
and no other stone, tipped and figured
with flowers, each petal a perfect gem.
She wore no other decoration
in her hair which in its falling framed
a face as white as ivory
and noble in its gravity.
Like hand-worked gold her fine hair shone
and flowed unbound around her shoulders,
the chalk-white pallor of her skin as pure
as all the fine-set pearls she wore.

Where her skin met the white of the linen
at her wrists, her throat and on every hem,
there were pearls, palest of all the stones.
Her whole dress shone like an icy stream
and there at the heart of it all on her breast
lay a single immaculate pearl far greater
than all the rest. To tell its true measure
or worth would test a man's mind to the limit.
I swear no singer however inspired
could find words to describe the sight
of that pearl, so perfect, so faultless, so pale,
placed in the most precious setting of all.

I watched as this darling creature set
with pearls walked at the water's edge
toward me: no man was happier from here
to Greece at the moment she came so near.
For the girl was dearer to my heart
than aunt or niece and the love I felt
for her far deeper. Inclining her head
with all the grace of a lady she bowed,
took off her jewel-encrusted crown
and with joy in her voice she greeted me.
That I had lived to speak to her
was heaven itself. My pearl, my girl.

GARNET ∘∘ CARNELIAN ∘∘∘ PEARL ∘∘∘ TOPAZ ∘∘ AQUAMARINE ∘∘ RUBY ∘∘ AGATE ∘∘∘ DIAMOND ∘∘ JADE ∘∘

A Beading of Words
Eithne Cavanagh

I beaded your words
around my summer-tanned ankle,
even tried them on my toes
not comfortable.

But these were just the bauble words.

Real meanings, clouded as opal,
you misered in a hidden place
forcing me to search, excavate
for what I craved.

Understanding, I adorned myself,
put your words on my fingers,
around my neck, flaunting gleefully
these utterings from your soul

to harbour as my own.

Nursery Rhymes
Traditional

Ride a cock horse to Banbury Cross
To see a fine lady upon a white horse
With rings on her fingers and bells on her toes
She shall have music wherever she goes.

I had a little nut-tree
Nothing would it bear,
But a silver nutmeg
And a golden pear.

The King of Spain's daughter
Came to visit me,
And all for the sake
Of my little nut-tree.

Little girl, little girl where have you been?
Gathering roses to give to the Queen.
Little girl, little girl what gave she you?
She gave me a diamond as big as my shoe.

Here Is The Bracelet

Louisa May Alcott (1832-1888)

Here is the bracelet
For good little May
To wear on her arm
By night and by day.
When it shines like the sun,
All's going well;
But when you are bad,
A sharp prick will tell.
Farewell, little girl,
For now we must part.
Make a fairy-box, dear,
Of your own happy heart;
And take out for all
Sweet gifts every day,
Till all the year round
Is like beautiful May.

Precious Stones
Christina Rossetti (1830-1894)

An emerald is as green as grass,
A ruby red as blood,
A sapphire shines as blue as heaven,
But a flint lies in the mud.

A diamond is a brilliant stone
To catch the world's desire,
An opal holds a rainbow light,
But a flint holds fire.

The Choice

Dorothy Parker (1893-1967)

He'd have given me rolling lands,
    Houses of marble, and billowing farms,
Pearls, to trickle between my hands,
    Smoldering rubies, to circle my arms.
You–you'd only a lilting song,
    Only a melody, happy and high,
You were sudden and swift and strong–
    Never a thought for another had I.

He'd have given me laces rare,
    Dresses that glimmered with frosty sheen,
Shining ribbons to wrap my hair,
    Horses to draw me, as fine as a queen.
You–you'd only to whistle low,
    Gayly I followed wherever you led.
I took you, and I let him go–
    Somebody ought to examine my head!

Birthstones
Traditional

By her who in this month (January) is born
No gem save *garnets* shall be worn;
They will ensure her constancy,
True friendship, and fidelity.

The February-born shall find
Sincerity and peace of mind,
Freedom from passion and from care,
If they an *amethyst* will wear.

Who in this world of ours their eyes
In March first open shall be wise,
In days of peril firm and brave,
And wear a *bloodstone* to their grave.

She who from April dates her years,
Diamonds shall wear, lest bitter tears
For vain repentance flow; this stone,
Emblem of innocence, is known.

Who first beholds the light of day
In spring's sweet flowery month of May
And wears an *emerald* all her life
Shall be a loved and happy wife.

Who comes with summer to this earth,
And owes to June her hour of birth,
With ring of *agate* on her hand
Can health, wealth, and long life command.

The gleaming *ruby* shall adorn,
Those who in July are born;
Then they'll be exempt and free
From love's doubts and anxiety.

Wear a *sardonyx* or for thee,
No conjugal felicity;
The August-born without this stone,
'Tis said, must live unloved and lone.

A maiden born when September leaves
Are rustling in September's breeze,
A *sapphire* on her brow should bind
'Twill cure diseases of the mind.

October's child is born for woe,
And life's vicissitudes must know,
But lay an *opal* on her breast,
And hope will lull those woes to rest.

Who first comes to this world below
With drear November's fog and snow,
Should prize the *topaz*'s amber hue,
Emblem of friends and lovers true.

If cold December gave you birth,
The month of snow and ice and mirth,
Place on your hand a *turquoise* blue;
Success will bless whate'er you do.

The Gregorian calendar has poems matching each month with its birthstone. Tiffany & Co published these poems "of unknown author" for the first time in a pamphlet in 1870.

For the Shop

C P Cavafy (1863-1933)

Carefully, neatly he folded them between
Wrappings of silk, expensive, fine and green.

Rubies like roses, pearls made into lilies,
And amethystine violets. As his will is,

He made, and sees them fair; not as he has known
Or noted nature. In the safe they're thrown,

Proof of his daring workmanship and skill.
A buyer comes into the shop; he'll still

Sell from their cases other pretty things –
Bracelets, and chains, and necklaces and rings.

Nothing

James Fenton

I take a jewel from a junk-shop tray
And I wish I had a love to buy it for.
Nothing I choose will make you turn my way.
Nothing I give will make you love me more.

I know that I've embarrassed you too long
And I'm ashamed to linger at your door.
Whatever I embark on will be wrong.
Nothing I do will make you love me more.

I cannot work. I cannot read or write.
How can I frame a letter to implore.
Eloquence is a lie. The truth is trite.
Nothing I say will make you love me more.

So I replace the jewel in the tray
And laughingly pretend I'm far too poor.
Nothing I give, nothing I do or say,
Nothing I am will make you love me more.

Whitby Jet
Sally Evans

Black stone soft to carve
beads, ornament, brooches.
Stone, fine and intricate,
to wear, to revel in,
and slowly break.

Below gull torn skies
in the fishing town,
by Staithes, under quayside sails,
the sharp glitter, a dark rainbow
in booths.

Night flowering, a perennial glow
of east coast darkness, the poet-monk
Caedmon's fire.

Welsh Gold

Gillian Clarke

Two thousand years ago, before
he knew the word for *aurum, aur,*
a man was lured by a single yellow hair,
into the-gods-knew-where
of the underworld.
A sun-struck thread in rock,
filament of lightning, electric shock,
Apollo's pollens alchemised to gold.

A thousand years ago
in the scriptorium at Ystrad Flûr
a monk scribing his way across the page
a line of verse in Welsh from the Age
of Poets, heard a blackbird, clear
in the branches of an oak,
and dipping its feather in gold
touched an initial with a masterstroke.

Here, in the mine, a trace
gleams on the worked rock face
like a line of verse on the wall,
a shaft of meaning, then illegible.
The gold has all but gone, its alchemy
undone like the illusion of money.

Sunlight on the river is fools' gold.
The real stuff's stored
in human muscle, blood and bone,
and an unrecoverable hoard
slips through our hands in the sea.

Blue Glass
Fleur Adcock

The underworld of children becomes the overworld
when Janey or Sharon shuts the attic door
on a sunny afternoon and tiptoes in sandals
that softly waffle-print the dusty floor

to the cluttered bed below the skylight,
managing not to sneeze as she lifts
newspapers, boxes, gap-stringed tennis-racquets
and a hamster's cage to the floor and shifts

the tasselled cover to make a clean surface
and a pillow to be tidy under her head
before she straightens, mouths the dark sentence,
and lays herself out like a mummy on the bed.

Her wrists are crossed. The pads of her fingertips
trace the cold glass emblem where it lies
like a chain of hailstones melting in the dips
above her collarbones. She needs no eyes

to see it: the blue bead necklace, of sapphire
or lapis, or of other words she knows
which might mean blueness: amethyst, azure,
chalcedony can hardly say how it glows.

She stole it. She tells herself that she found it.
It's hers now. It owns her. She slithers among
its globular teeth, skidding on blue pellets.
Ice-beads flare and blossom on her tongue,

turn into flowers, populate the spaces
around and below her. The attic has become
her bluebell wood. Among their sappy grasses
the light-fringed gas-flames of bluebells hum.

They lift her body like a cloud of petals.
High now, floating, this is what she sees:
granular bark six inches from her eyeballs;
the wood of rafters is the wood of trees.

Her breathing moistens the branches' undersides;
the sunlight in an interrupted shaft
warms her legs and lulls her as she rides
on air, a slender and impossible raft

of bones and flesh; and whether it is knowledge
or a limpid innocence on which she feeds
for power hasn't mattered. She turns the necklace
kindly in her fingers, and soothes the beads.

The Uncut Diamond
Robert Graves (1895-1985)

This is ours by natural, not by civil, right:
An uncut diamond, found while picnicking
Beside blue clay here on the open veldt!
It should carve up to a walnut-sized brilliant
And a score of lesser gems.

What shall we do? To be caught smuggling stones
Assures us each a dozen years in gaol;
And who can trust a cutting-agency?
So, do you love me?
                      Or must I toss it back?

The Diamond Cutter
Elizabeth Jennings (1926-2001)

Not what the light will do but how he shapes it
And what particular colours it will bear,

And something of the climber's concentration,
Seeing the white peak, setting the right foot there.

Not how the sun was plausible at morning
Nor how it was distributed at noon

And not how much the single stone could show
But rather how much brilliance it would shun;

Simply a paring down, a cleaving to
One object, as the star-gazer who sees

One single comet polished by its fall
Rather than countless, untouched galaxies.

from **Morte d'Arthur**
Alfred Tennyson (1809-1892)

There drew he forth the brand Excalibur,
And o'er him, drawing it, the winter moon,
Brightening the skirts of a long cloud, ran forth
And sparkled keen with frost against the hilt:
For all the haft twinkled with diamond sparks,
Myriads of topaz-lights, and jacinth work
Of subtlest jewellery. He gazed so long
That both his eyes were dazzled, as he stood,
This way and that dividing the swift mind,
In act to throw: but at the last it seem'd
Better to leave Excalibur conceal'd
There in the many-knotted water-flags,
That whistled stiff and dry about the marge.
So strode he back slow to the wounded King.

from **Romaunt of the Rose**
Geoffrey Chaucer (1343-1400)

Richesse a robe of purpre on hadde,
...
And with a bend of gold tasseled,
And knoppes *(ornamental knobs)* fyne of gold ameled.
Aboute hir nekke of gentil entaile *(workmanship)*
Was shet the riche chevesaile *(necklace)*,
In which ther was ful gret plentee
Of stones clere and bright to see.
Richesse a girdel hadde upon,
The bokel of it was of a stoon
Of vertu greet, ...
The barres *(part of a buckle)* were of gold ful fyne,
Upon a tissu of satyne,
Ful hevy, greet, and no-thing light,
In everich was a besaunt-wight *(weight)*.
Upon the tresses of Richesse
Was set a cercle, for noblesse,
Of brend *(burnished)* gold, that ful lighte shoon;
So fair, trowe I, was never noon.
But he were cunning, for the nones *(well skilled)*,
That coude devysen alle the stones
That in that cercle shewen clere;
It is a wonder thing to here.
For no man coude preyse *(value)* or gesse
Of hem the valewe or richesse.
Rubyes there were, saphyres, iagounces *(jacinths)*,
And emeraudes, more than two ounces.

Rings
Carol Ann Duffy

for both to say

I might have raised your hand to the sky
to give you the ring surrounding the moon
or looked to twin the rings of your eyes
with mine
or added a ring to the rings of a tree
by forming a handheld circle with you, thee,
or walked with you
where a ring of church-bells,
looped the fields,
or kissed a lipstick ring on your cheek,
a pressed flower,
or met with you
in the ring of an hour,
and another hour ...
I might
have opened your palm to the weather, turned, turned,
till your fingers were ringed in rain
or held you close,
they were playing our song,
in the ring of a slow dance
or carved our names
in the rough ring of a heart
or heard the ring of an owl's hoot
as we headed home in the dark
or the ring, first thing,
of chorussing birds
waking the house
or given the ring of a boat, rowing the lake,
or the ring of swans, monogamous, two,

or the watery rings made by the fish
as they leaped and splashed
or the ring of the sun's reflection there ...
I might have tied
a blade of grass,
a green ring for your finger,
or told you the ring of a sonnet by heart
or brought you a lichen ring,
found on a warm wall,
or given a ring of ice in winter
or in the snow
sung with you the five gold rings of a carol
or stolen a ring of your hair
or whispered the word in your ear
that brought us here,
where nothing and no one is wrong,
and therefore I give you this ring.

A Lost Jewel

Robert Graves (1895-1985)

Who on your breast pillows his head now,
Jubilant to have won
The heart beneath on fire for him alone,

At dawn will hear you, plagued by nightmare,
Mumble and weep
About some blue jewel you were sworn to keep.

Wake, blink, laugh out in reassurance,
Yet your tears will say,
"It was not mine to lose or give away.

"For love it shone, never for the madness
Of a strange bed–
Light on my finger, fortune in my head."

Roused by your naked grief and beauty,
For lust he will burn:
"Turn to me, sweetheart! Why do you not turn?"

Brooch Found at Redcar

Sally Evans

Redcar, a hinterland,
unlandmarked coast of sand,

flat sea, small dunes, but yonder,
in un-grassed Saxon graves,

a brooch, a bullion find,
worked gold, red stone, a wonder

of burnished art. A hand
might hold the contraband

that gives back to this town
twelve centuries of depth

in such fine contour. Found,
truth's road we can go down,

marauding yarls behind
the quiet field around.

from **The Eve of St Agnes**
John Keats (1795-1821)

XXV

Full on this casement shone the wintry moon,
And threw warm gules on Madeline's fair breast,
As down she knelt for heaven's grace and boon;
Rose-bloom fell on her hands, together prest,
And on her silver cross soft amethyst,
And on her hair a glory, like a saint:
She seem'd a splendid angel, newly drest,
Save wings, for heaven:—Porphyro grew faint:
She knelt, so pure a thing, so free from mortal taint.

XXVI

Anon his heart revives: her vespers done,
Of all its wreathed pearls her hair she frees;
Unclasps her warmed jewels one by one;
Loosens her fragrant boddice; by degrees
Her rich attire creeps rustling to her knees:
Half-hidden, like a mermaid in sea-weed,
Pensive awhile she dreams awake, and sees,
In fancy, fair St. Agnes in her bed,
But dares not look behind, or all the charm is fled.

Rich and Rare Were the Gems She Wore
Thomas Moore (1779-1852)

Rich and rare were the gems she wore,
And a bright gold ring on her wand she bore;
But, O, her beauty was far beyond
Her sparkling gems or snow-white wand.

"Lady! dost thou not fear to stray,
So lone and lovely, through this bleak way?
Are Erin's sons so good or so cold
As not to be tempted by woman or gold?"

"Sir Knight! I feel not the least alarm,
No son of Erin will offer me harm;
For though they love woman and golden store,
Sir Knight! they love honour and virtue more!"

On she went, and her maiden smile
In safety lighted her round the green isle;
And blest forever is she who relied
Upon Erin's honour and Erin's pride!

From the footnotes of Irish Melodies:

This ballad is founded upon the following anecdote: "we are informed that a young lady of great beauty, adorned with jewels and a costly dress, undertook a journey alone, from one end of the kingdom to the other, with a wand only in her hand, at the top of which was a ring of exceeding great value; and such an impression had the laws and government of this Monarch (Brien) made on the minds of all the people, that no attempt was made upon her honour, nor was she robbed of her clothes or jewels." Warner's History of Ireland, vol. i., book x

Nacre

Ruth Fainlight

I Pearls
I
What other gem grows in a living creature
underwater

is made from crystalline substance
iridescent nacre

layer upon layer secreted, exuded
by the mantle's tissue

when one small grain of sand or parasite
embeds in the pulpy flesh

that fills a mollusc shell, to coat the irritant
and form a pearl.

II
Sometimes this happens – but rarely.
And few have much value. The magnificent pearls,
with their orient nacre, were saved
for queens and emperors. Entire villages
holding their breath: how many divers' lives
lost in the oyster beds for a royal crown?

III
Caligula named his horse a consul
then garlanded it with pearls.
Cleopatra, to flaunt her power
before Mark Anthony, dissolved
a pearl, the worth of a king's ransom,
in a glass of wine and swallowed it.
With one of his mother's pearl earrings,
General Vittelius
financed his most ambitious campaign.

IV
To decide if she would visit him,
Sheba set riddles to test Solomon.
Across the Red Sea and the desert,
in an envoy's sealed wallet,
among the other presents
she sent a hollowed moonstone
and an unpierced pearl.

Pearls were Krishna's wedding gift to his girl,
and part of Hindu marriage ritual
is the piercing of an undrilled pearl.

V Clam Chowder
II
But when lunch was over
and the plates washed up,
and she changed her dress
for the Ladies' Club,
I thought she looked best
if she wore that brooch
with a pearl in the centre
that had been her mother's,
and the pearl ear-studs.

In Memory of a Beautiful Jeweller
Kit Wright

Within the crescent of your jeweller's bench,
Nothing of all the intricate things you made
More beautiful than the shining
Necklace of your laughter,

Linking the days. Within the days,

Nothing of any rarer,
More precious metal than were you,
Loving and strong and brave
And capable and true.

String of Pearls

Leysa Lowery

Covered with the road map
Of a life well-lived,
Her tired, soft hands count the
Pearls knotted onto the string in her lap.
Her eyes, blinded by age,
See the memories
Filling her head, her heart.
Her lips move silently
Mouthing the names
Of loved ones lost,
In a prayer-like celebration
As she counts the pearls
Before her.
Her mother, who loved her first,
Her father, who loved her protectively.
Her husband, who loved her faithfully.
Her children, a son and two daughters,
Who loved her timelessly.
Friends, from childhood to old age,
Who loved through good times and bad.
A minister, who loved her as his
Bible taught.
A neighbour, who loved her, sharing
Conversation and coffee.
Grandchildren, who loved her
With simple honesty.
Each name dearly recalled as
Her fingers slip over the nacre's
Smooth surfaces.
A string of loves
Tied into the endless circle
Of one woman's life.
True treasure.

A Bracelet
Robert Graves (1895-1985)

A bracelet invisible
For your busy wrist,
Twisted from silver
Spilt afar,
From silver of the clear Moon,
From her sheer halo,
From the male beauty
Of a shooting star.

The Invisible Mender (My First Mother)
Sarah Maguire

I'm sewing on new buttons
to this washed silk shirt.
Mother-of-pearl,
I chose them carefully.
In the haberdasher's on Chepstow Place
I turned a boxful over
one by one,
searching for the backs with flaws:
those blemished green or pink or aubergine,
small birth marks on the creamy shell.

These afternoons are short,
the sunlight buried after three or four,
sap in the cold earth.
The trees are bare.
I'm six days late.
My right breast aches so
when I bend to catch a fallen button
that strays across the floor.
Either way
there'll be blood on my hands.

Thirty-seven years ago you sat in poor light
and sewed your time away.

We Alone

Alice Walker

We alone can devalue gold
by not caring
if it falls or rises
in the marketplace.
Wherever there is gold
there is a chain, you know,
and if your chain
is gold
so much the worse
for you.
Feathers, shells,
and sea-shaped stones
are all as rare.

This could be our revolution:
To love what is plentiful
as much as
what is scarce.

Overheard on a Saltmarsh

Harold Monro (1879-1932)

Nymph, nymph, what are your beads?

Green glass, goblin. Why do you stare at them?

Give them me.

No.

Give them me. Give them me.

No.

Then I will howl all night in the reeds,
lie in the mud and howl for them.

Goblin, why do you love them so?

They are better than stars or water,
Better than voices of winds that sing,
Better than any man's fair daughter,
Your green glass beads on a silver ring.

Hush, I stole them out of the moon.

Give me your beads, I want them.

No.

I will howl in a deep lagoon
For your green glass beads, I love them so.
Give them me. Give them.

No.

from **Two Bracelets**
Tess Gallagher

I wear on my left arm – one
of silver, the other gold.

I am your silver.
You are my gold.
My gold in you.
In me, your silver.

When I slip on my dress
in the morning, when I take it off
in the dark, my gold
clicks against your silver.
I hear it in my farthest
cave. You hear it
wherever you are and pause
as if a wing-shadow
had passed over your heart.

Of Diamonds
Matthew Francis

There are many Indias. This one is hard and cold.
Water freezes to ice, and ice becomes petrified
to crystal. On the rocks of crystal, diamonds grow,

feeding on frost and the scant sunlight, male and female
engendering smaller diamonds after their kind.
If you pull one up by the roots, with some of its bed,

keep it and water it, it grows a little each year,
brooding on its colours like a dragon on its hoard,
or spitting them into the air in Platonic sparks.

Beware of lesser stones in disguise. If offered one,
test with a magnet and needle – it should kill their love.
When poison is nearby, it grows cold and starts to sweat.

Wear a diamond on the left side of your body
and no vicious or venomous creature will harm you.
It protects against lunacy, witchcraft and nightmares.

But if you misbehave it shrinks back into a rock
until a worthier owner comes to cosset it.
You must live up to it. Its morals are mineral.

The Bracelet: To Julia

Robert Herrick (1591-1674)

Why I tie about thy wrist,
Julia, this silken twist;
For what other reason 'tis
But to show thee how, in part,
Thou my pretty captive art?
But thy bond slave is my heart:
'tis but silk that bindeth thee,
Knap the thread and thou art free;
But 'tis otherwise with me:
-I am bound and fast bound, so
That from thee I cannot go;
If I could, I would not so.

from **The Odyssey (Book 18)**
Homer
Translated by Robert Fagles (1933-2008)

(The suitors' gifts for Penelope)

Each suitor sent a page to go and get a gift.
Antinous' man brought in a grand, resplendent robe,
stiff with embroidery, clasped with twelve gold brooches,
long pins that clipped into sheathing loops with ease.
Eurymachus' man brought in a necklace richly wrought,
gilded, strung with amber and glowing like the sun.
Eurydamas' two men came with a pair of earrings,
mulberry clusters dangling in triple drops
with a glint to catch the heart.
From the halls of lord Pisander, Polyctor's son,
a servant brought a choker, a fine, gleaming treasure.
And so each suitor in turn laid on a handsome gift.
Then the noble queen withdrew to her upper room,
her file of waiting ladies close behind her,
bearing the gorgeous presents in their arms.

Jewellery
Robert Melliard

They never bought each other diamonds,
rubies, sapphires, pearls or gold.

The only precious things they keep
are memories of days they spent:
on golden coasts with turquoise seas;
or viewing snow-enamelled peaks;
tangled up in bed;
or simply playing with their children;
or dining out with friends.

Jewels in my hand

Sasha Moorsom (1931-1993)

I hold dead friends like jewels in my hand
Watching their brilliance gleam against my palm
Turquoise and emerald, jade, a golden band

All ravages of time they can withstand
Like talismans their grace keeps me from harm
I hold dead friends like jewels in my hand

I see them standing in some borderland
Their heads half-turned, waiting for my arm
Turquoise and emerald, jade, a golden band

I'm not afraid they will misunderstand
My turning to them like a magic charm
I hold dead friends like jewels in my hand
Turquoise and emerald, jade, a golden band.

Acknowledgements

We would like to thank Neil Morgan and Jon Buckingham for their help and support in publishing this collection.

We would also like to thank the following artists and poets for permission to publish their work: Harry Brockway, Josie Brown, Colette Bryce (The Wearer was commissioned by the V&A Museum, 2002, to celebrate the British Galleries 1500-1900), Eithne Cavanagh, Sally Evans, Anita Klein (www.anitaklein.com/www.anitaklein.co.uk), Leysa Lowery, Robert Melliard, Alice Patullo, Victoria Redel, Alicia Stubbersfield, Alasdair Watson.

We gratefully acknowledge permission to reprint copyright material in this book as follows: Painting Shah Jahan holding a jewel by Muhammad Abed © Victoria and Albert Museum; Blue Glass from Poems 1960-2000 by Fleur Adcock (Bloodaxe Books 2000); Presents from my Aunts in Pakistan from Split World: Poems 1990-2005 by Moniza Alvi (Bloodaxe Books 2008); The Book of Matches by Simon Armitage (Faber and Faber Ltd); Chain necklace with peacock pendant designed by Charles Robert Ashbee © Victoria and Albert Museum, London; Angela Burdett-Coutts (Wellcome Library, London); Amber from Five Fields by Gillian Clarke (Carcanet Press Ltd 1998); Welsh Gold from Recipe for Water by Gillian Clarke (Carcanet Press Ltd 2009); The Flowering of the Rod from Collected Poems 1912-44 by Hilda Doolittle (Carcanet Press Ltd 1984); Extract from Pearl by Jane Draycott (Carcanet Press Ltd 2011); Warming her Pearls from Selling Manhattan by Carol Ann Duffy (Anvil Press Poetry 1987); Rings from The Bees by Carol Ann Duffy (Picador 2011) © Carol Ann Duffy 2011, reproduced by permission of the author c/o Rogers, Coleridge & White Ltd, 20 Powis Mews, London W11 1JN; Greek Beads from Out of the Blue: 1975-2001 by Helen Dunmore (Bloodaxe Books 2001); Brooch from Perfect Blemish: New and Selected Poems 1995-2007 by Menna Elfyn (Bloodaxe Books 2007); A Game of Chess from The Wasteland by T S Eliot (Faber and Faber Ltd); Nacre from New and Collected Poems by Ruth Fainlight (Bloodaxe Books 2010); Nothing from Yellow Tulips by James Fenton (Faber and Faber Ltd); Of Diamonds from Mandeville by Matthew Francis (Faber and Faber Ltd); Tess Gallagher, excerpt from Two Bracelets from Midnight Lantern: New and Selected Poems © 1995 by Tess Gallagher reprinted with the permission of The Permissions Co Inc on behalf of Greywolf Press, Minneapolis, Minnesota, www. greywolfpress.org; The Necklace, The Uncut Diamond, A Lost Jewel and A Bracelet from Complete Poems in One Volume by Robert Graves (Carcanet Press Ltd 2000); Book 18: The Beggar-King of Ithaca from The Odyssey by Homer trans by Robert Fagles © 1996 by Robert Fagles, by permission of Viking Penguin, a division of Penguin Group (USA) Inc; The Locket from Collected Poems by Ted Hughes (Faber and Faber Ltd); The Brooch from The Tree House by Kathleen Jamie (Picador 2004); The Diamond Cutter from Collected Poems by Elizabeth Jennings (Carcanet Press Ltd 2012); My Grandmother's Opal from Selected Poems by Grevel Lindop (Carcanet Press Ltd 2000); The Invisible Mender from The Invisible Mender by Sarah Maguire (Jonathan Cape 1997) reprinted by permission of The Random House Group Ltd; Jeweller's Shop, from Lapidaire de Mandeville, French School, (15th century)/Bibliotheque Nationale/The Bridgeman Art Library; Les Bijoux, drawing by Lucien Métivet engraved on wood by G Lemoine from Clair de Lune by Guy de Maupassant, Paris 1905; Jewels in my hand from Your Head in Mine by Sasha Moorsom (Carcanet Press Ltd 1994); Woman at Kitchen Table by Philip Gregory Needell (1886-1974)/Abbott and Holder/The Bridgeman Art Library; Opals from Tell Me This is Normal: New and Selected Poems by Julie O'Callaghan (Bloodaxe Books 2008); The Choice from The Best of Dorothy Parker (Gerald Duckworth & Co Ltd); King Arthur and the Weeping Queens wood engraving by Dalziel brothers after Dante Gabriel Rossetti from Poems by Alfred Tennyson (Edward Moxon 1857); We Alone from Collected Poems by Alice Walker (Orion 2005); In Memory of a Beautiful Jeweller from The Magic Box by Kit Wright (Macmillan Children's Books, London, UK 2013).

Every effort has been made to trace or contact all copyright holders. The publishers would be pleased to rectify any omissions brought to their notice at the earliest opportunity.

Postscript

These pearls of thought in Persian gulfs were bred,
Each softly lucent as a rounded moon;
The diver Omar plucked them from their bed,
FitzGerald strung them on an English thread.

James Russell Lowell (describing the Rubaiyat of Omar Khayyam)

Poetry, the highest achievement of Persian literature, has been likened to setting jewels in wrought gold, or, as one of the words used in Persian to mean poetry, *naẓm*, signifies, stringing the pearls of meaning on the thread of rhyme.

...

Royal patrons were expected to reward poets richly for laudatory verse or other works dedicated to them. The poets could expect money, acclaim, a robe of honour, and even for their mouths to be stuffed full of precious jewels in return for their jewel-like verses.

From Bodleian exhibition *Love and Devotion: From Persia and Beyond*.
Alasdair Watson, Curator of Islamic Manuscripts at the Bodleian Library

This portrait of Shah Jahan (1628-1658) is signed by the court artist Muhammad Abed. The portrait depicts Shah Jahan, a renowned connoisseur of precious stones, wearing necklaces, bracelets, armlets and turban jewels made of very large pearls, spinels and emeralds. He holds a huge, facetted emerald in his left hand.

تصویر شاه جهان

EMERALD · GOLD · SAPPHIRE · AMBER · PEARL · TURQUOISE · OPAL · SILVER · CORAL